COLLEGE SPORTS TODAY

COLLEGE SPORTS TODAY

RUNNING RENEGADE!

THE FLORIDA STATE SEMINOLES STORY

NEAL BERNARDS

CREATIVE EDUCATION

Published by Creative Education
123 South Broad Street, Mankato, Minnesota 56001
Creative Education is an imprint of The Creative Company

Designed by Stephanie Blumenthal
Production design by The Design Lab
Editorial assistance by John Nichols

Photos by: Allsport USA, AP/Wide World Photos, Archive Photos,
SportsChrome, and UPI/Corbis-Bettmann

Library of Congress Cataloging-in-Publication Data

Bernards, Neal, 1963–
Running renegade! the Florida State Seminoles story / by Neal Bernards.
p. cm. — (College football today)
Summary: Highlights some of the important personalities and key moments
in football played at Florida State University.
ISBN: 0-88682-977-1

1. Florida State Seminoles (Football team)—History—Juvenile literature. 2. Florida State University—
Football—History—Juvenile literature. [1. Florida State Seminoles (Football team)—History.
2. Football—History.] I. Title. II. Series: College football today (Mankato, Minn.)

GV958.F55B47   1999
796.323'63'0975988—dc21   98-46471

First Edition

2 4 6 8 9 7 5 3 1

It's gameday in Doak Campbell Stadium in Tallahassee, Florida, and 80,000 charged-up, cheering fans are on their feet as the Florida State University football team takes the field. The roar becomes deafening as Chief Osceola, riding his majestic steed Renegade, plants a flaming spear in the turf at midfield. It is a sign to all in the stadium that there will be no escape for opponents, who are about to experience the fury of Seminoles football firsthand. Like a garnet and gold tidal wave, the 'Noles have rolled over opponents with alarming regularity. Since 1980, FSU has won an incredible 82 percent of their games. The Seminoles' style of play is simple: attack, attack, and attack some more. Florida State's brand of full-speed-ahead football leaves opponents bruised, beaten, and anxious for retreat.

COACH BOBBY BOWDEN HAS

MADE FLORIDA STATE A

FOOTBALL POWERHOUSE.

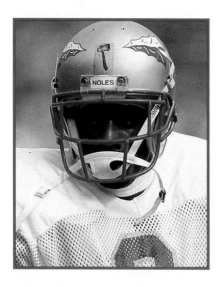

FORGING A WINNER

Florida State is located in Tallahassee, the state's capital city and home to 120,000 people. Tallahassee sits in the panhandle of Florida, just 20 miles from the Gulf of Mexico and 14 miles from the Georgia border. This old city, founded in 1824, is characterized by rolling hills, moss-draped oaks, and a rich history that links it more to the pre-Civil War south than to such modern cities as Orlando with Disney World and Miami with its beaches, condominiums, and fancy hotels.

1947 marked the first year of FSU and its football program. After World War II had come to an end, thousands of young men returned to college after serving in the U.S. military. To handle the sudden crush of male applicants, the school, then known as Florida State College for Women, decided to open its doors to men as well and changed its name to "Florida State University." Since that time, FSU has developed into a well-respected research university that is home to 30,000 students from all parts of the world.

Florida State was so quick to admit men in 1947 that it forgot to pick a nickname for its football team. After their nameless team played two games, Florida State students voted to become known as the "Seminoles," in honor of the Native American tribe that has inhabited Florida for centuries. It is their spear that decorates both sides of the Florida State football helmet.

THE SEMINOLES HELMET IS AN INTIMIDATING SIGHT.

Florida State's football team had a name, but little else. In its first season, the team of 45 volunteer players had no stadium and no scholarships. Ed Williamson, FSU's first head football coach, drew no pay for coaching the team. During that first campaign, the Seminoles posted an 0–5 record against such opponents as Stetson, Cumberland, and Jacksonville State. Despite his team's poor record and lack of resources, 1947 letterwinner Bill Bishop recalled that the Seminoles played with pride. "We just were happy to be playing ball," he said.

Coach Williamson stepped down after the season, and new coach Don Veller led FSU to a 7–1 mark the next year. In 1949, the Seminoles went 9–1 and earned a berth in their first bowl game, the Cigar Bowl in Tampa, Florida. In that game, the upstart Seminoles set the tone for future FSU squads, beating Wofford 19–6 with two touchdown runs from Red Parrish and 132 rushing yards from Buddy Strauss.

By 1952, Florida State had graduated to playing a major college schedule, and by the end of the '50s, the school had appeared in two more bowl games and established itself as a competitive program.

"STICKUM" FRED

With the start of the 1960s, Florida State began a second stage of rapid improvement. New head coach Bill "Pete" Peterson told the players on his 1960 team that it was their job to take FSU football to a new level. "Coach Peterson

was a prideful man," all-purpose offensive threat Bud Whitehead recalled. "A lot of times, it seemed he just willed us to win."

Seminoles fans did see a lot of winning under Peterson. His teams went 62–42–11 with four bowl appearances during his 11 seasons in Tallahassee. One of Peterson's prize pupils was a painfully unathletic-looking receiver from Erie, Pennsylvania, named Fred Biletnikoff. Biletnikoff was neither big, nor fast, nor strong. Yet he became Florida State's first consensus All-American player in 1964.

Although Biletnikoff didn't have great strength or speed, he did have an amazing knack for eluding defenders with a slight head fake, drop of the shoulder, or shifting of the feet. Biletnikoff was known for running precise pass patterns and for always finding a way to get open.

Sportswriter Leigh Montville described Biletnikoff as "a slow-motion, pass-catching perfectionist." Even Fred could joke about his lack of speed. "Any person on the field can catch me from behind," he once commented. "That includes the officials."

Biletnikoff's career at Florida State did not start quickly. He barely played in his first two years and had an average junior year. But during his senior season, Biletnikoff caught fire, hooking up with quarterback Steve Tensi for 57 catches and 11 touchdowns in 10 games. To cap his All-American season, the 6-foot-1 receiver

OFFENSIVE LINEMAN

ROBERT URICH

(ABOVE); COACH BILL

PETERSON (LEFT)

THE BRASH AND EXPLOSIVE DEION SANDERS

shredded the mighty Oklahoma Sooners in the 1965 Gator Bowl, catching 13 passes for 192 yards and four touchdowns, leading the Seminoles to a stunning, 36–19 victory.

After college, Biletnikoff enjoyed a brilliant, 13-year professional career with the powerful Oakland Raiders. During that time, he became known as the man with "stickum." He earned this label because he would cover his hands and uniform with a gooey, sticky substance that helped him hang on to the ball. Biletnikoff slathered the stuff on so thick that he could not touch anything. "You don't even touch the ground with your hands," he described with a smile. "You push yourself off the ground with your elbows because your hands are so sticky."

Regardless of how he did it, Biletnikoff made some amazing catches in his football career and became the first of 18 Florida State consensus All-Americans and a member of the Pro Football Hall of Fame in 1988.

BOBBY BOWDEN (ABOVE)

HAS CREATED EXCITEMENT

IN TALLAHASSEE FOR

MORE THAN 20 YEARS.

THE REIGN OF COACH BOWDEN

Bill Peterson put Florida State football on the map during the 1960s, but when he stepped down after the 1970 season, FSU's football fortunes sank like a stone. By 1976, the Seminoles' faithful had suffered through a three-season stretch that included only four wins.

Into this dire situation walked a 47-year-old miracle worker by the name of Bobby Bowden. To Florida

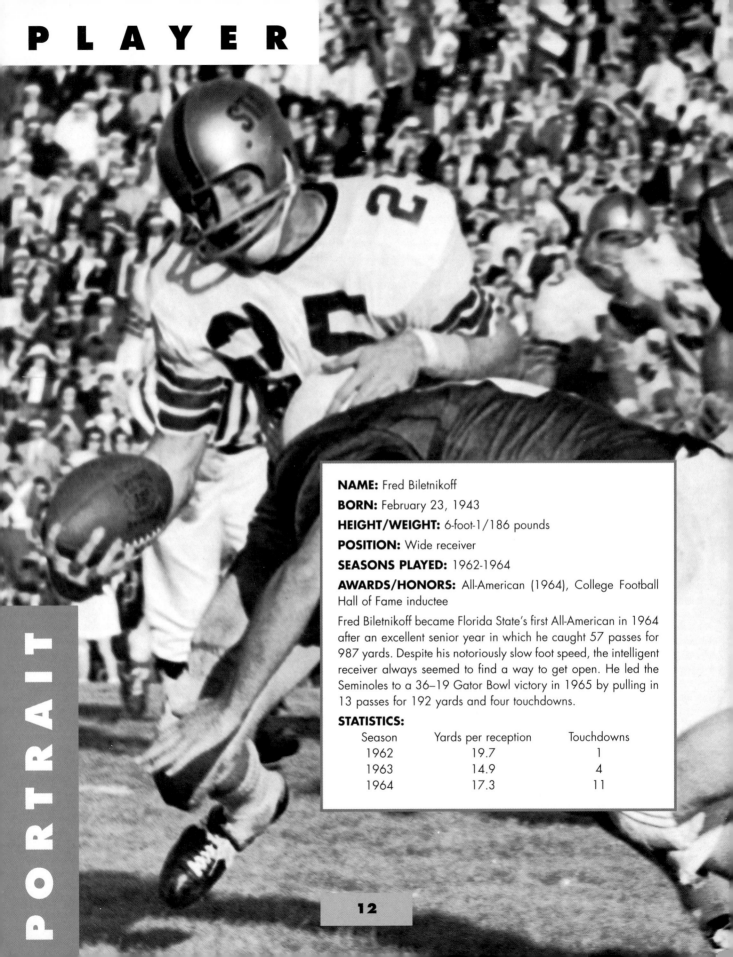

NAME: Fred Biletnikoff

BORN: February 23, 1943

HEIGHT/WEIGHT: 6-foot-1/186 pounds

POSITION: Wide receiver

SEASONS PLAYED: 1962-1964

AWARDS/HONORS: All-American (1964), College Football Hall of Fame inductee

Fred Biletnikoff became Florida State's first All-American in 1964 after an excellent senior year in which he caught 57 passes for 987 yards. Despite his notoriously slow foot speed, the intelligent receiver always seemed to find a way to get open. He led the Seminoles to a 36–19 Gator Bowl victory in 1965 by pulling in 13 passes for 192 yards and four touchdowns.

STATISTICS:

Season	Yards per reception	Touchdowns
1962	19.7	1
1963	14.9	4
1964	17.3	11

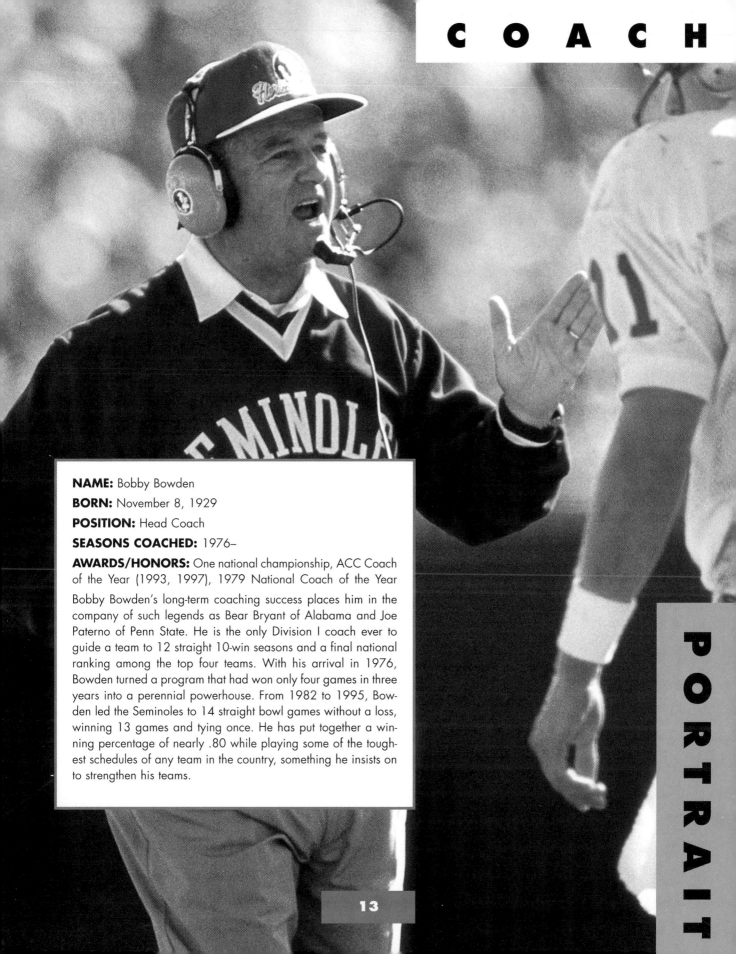

NAME: Bobby Bowden

BORN: November 8, 1929

POSITION: Head Coach

SEASONS COACHED: 1976–

AWARDS/HONORS: One national championship, ACC Coach of the Year (1993, 1997), 1979 National Coach of the Year

Bobby Bowden's long-term coaching success places him in the company of such legends as Bear Bryant of Alabama and Joe Paterno of Penn State. He is the only Division I coach ever to guide a team to 12 straight 10-win seasons and a final national ranking among the top four teams. With his arrival in 1976, Bowden turned a program that had won only four games in three years into a perennial powerhouse. From 1982 to 1995, Bowden led the Seminoles to 14 straight bowl games without a loss, winning 13 games and tying once. He has put together a winning percentage of nearly .80 while playing some of the toughest schedules of any team in the country, something he insists on to strengthen his teams.

PORTRAIT

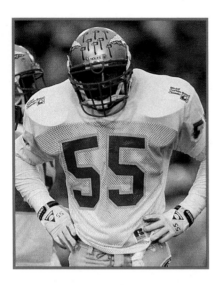

LINEBACKER MARVIN

JONES (ABOVE); ELUSIVE

TAILBACK WARRICK

DUNN (BELOW)

State fans, Coach Bowden *is* Seminoles football, a good ol' boy from Birmingham, Alabama, who can work his team into a pregame frenzy like a Southern Baptist preacher. The Seminoles' coach motivates, criticizes, and congratulates players like a father does a son.

Bowden developed his love of football in an unusual way. At age 13, young Bobby fell ill with rheumatic fever and was kept at home for a year. He spent long hours in bed listening to radio broadcasts of his favorite college teams in action. He also listened to reports coming from Europe about World War II. He loved diagraming the football plays he heard on the radio and mapping out the battles of a far-off war. That year away from the playground made him realize that he could enjoy a game without actually playing it.

Bowden starred as a quarterback at Woodlawn High School in Birmingham and played for one year at the University of Alabama. He started coaching in 1959 at Samford University and moved on to run a successful West Virginia program.

But when Bowden came to Florida State in 1976, things were tough. Years later, Bowden could joke about how bad the

BRAD JOHNSON WORE THE GARNET AND GOLD FROM 1988 TO 1991.

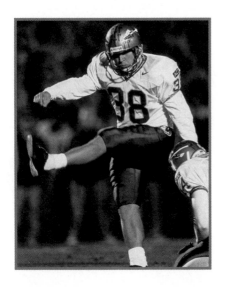

situation was. "When I was at West Virginia, all I heard was 'Beat Pitt' [the school's main rival]," he said. "When I got to Florida State, their bumper stickers read, 'Beat Anybody.'"

Bowden turned the program around in two years. In 1976, Florida State went 5–6. In 1977, led by All-American nose guard Ron Simmons and running back Larry Key, the 'Noles jumped to 10–2 and won the Tangerine Bowl. Bowden had quickly brought pride back to the Florida State program.

One of the main reasons for FSU's constant success over the years has been Bowden's innovative formations and play-calling. "Bobby's been at this since I was a kid," said Florida University coach Steve Spurrier. "And yet every year, I see something new and different from his teams. He's not afraid to change with the times, and he's always got something up his sleeve for you."

During his storied reign in Tallahassee, Bowden has coached such greats as defensive backs Leroy Butler and Terrell Buckley, defensive linemen Andre Wadsworth and Reinard Wilson, and linebackers Peter Boulware, Derrick Brooks, and Marvin Jones—all consensus All-Americans who became stars in the National Football League. Guiding such quality players, Bowden had captured nearly 300 victories and one national championship by the late 1990s.

TALLAHASSEE TRADITIONS

In addition to Florida State's long line of talented alumni, the school is also home to some of the proudest traditions in college football. Just before kickoff at all home games, a student dressed as the great Chief Osceola holds a flaming spear and charges down the field on an Appaloosa horse named Renegade. Then, just as the stadium seems ready to explode with the resounding cheers of the Seminoles' faithful, the Chief hurls his spear into the ground, planting a fiery warning to the opposing team.

In another football ritual, the Seminoles' players are awarded small tomahawk decals to wear on their helmets to recognize outstanding plays made on the field. Although many schools follow this practice, Florida State's tradition is a unique one that allows players to earn tomahawks for feats of academic excellence as well. "We wanted to stress that players should strive to do great things in all areas of the college experience," explained Bowden.

COACH BOWDEN (ABOVE);

FIERCE ALL-AMERICAN

CORNERBACK TERRELL

BUCKLEY (BELOW)

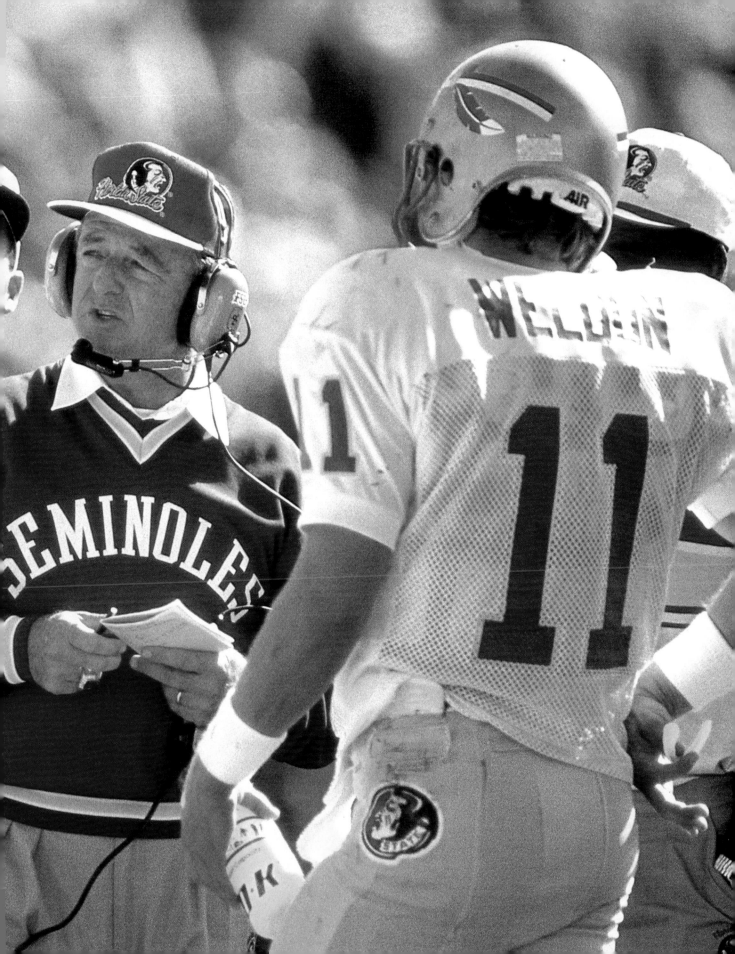

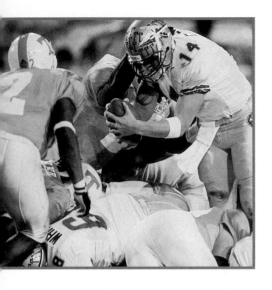

SEMINOLES QUARTER-

BACKS MARCUS OUTZEN

(ABOVE) AND CHARLIE

WARD (BELOW)

Perhaps Florida State's most interesting bit of tradition involves a small field where big 'Noles victories go to be buried. In a far corner of the team's practice field in Tallahassee, visitors can view a small "cemetery" erected by Florida State groundskeepers. But there are no bodies in this cemetery. It is the sod cemetery. Little pieces of opponents' fields are buried there to commemorate big wins at away games.

The sod cemetery was started in 1962 when a couple of FSU football captains brought home some turf from the University of Georgia after an 18–0 win. The piece of sod was buried in a corner of Florida State's practice field, and a monument was erected over the site. Since then, any big away-game wins or bowl-game victories are remembered by bringing home a bit of turf to bury in the cemetery. A small tombstone with the score and date of the win is then placed over the vanquished soil. When Seminoles' fans say that their team "buries" its opponents, they really mean it.

NEON DEION LIGHTS THE WAY

Coach Bowden always tells his recruiters to go out and sign the best athletes they can find. With Deion Sanders in 1985, FSU got an exceptional cornerback from Fort Myers, Florida, who took trash talking and boasting to a new level. But he was also a great athlete who lettered in football, baseball, and track at Florida State.

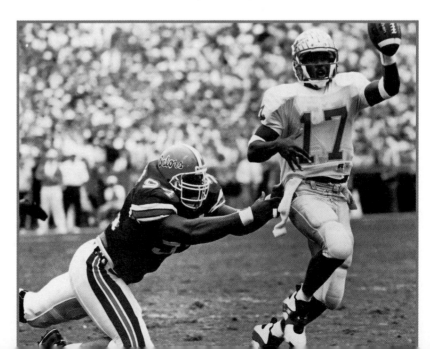

"Neon Deion" quickly became as well-known for his outrageous interviews as for his on-field play. He spoke his mind on any subject and drove opponents mad with a non-stop tirade of trash talking that continued for entire games. With Deion, however, the talk was backed up with action. Amazingly agile and blessed with blinding speed, the 6-foot-1 and 185-pound defensive back preyed on opposing quarterbacks. Sanders would often back away from receivers to make the passer think they were open. Then, once the ball was in the air, he would break back into the play with explosive speed, breaking up or intercepting the pass.

Once, in a road game against the Clemson Tigers, Sanders told the Tigers that he was going to run a punt back for a touchdown. After the Clemson players mocked him, Sanders returned the punt 76 yards for a touchdown. When he reached the end zone, he struck a pose and shouted to his opponents, "How you like me now?"

Coach Bowden did not encourage Sanders' antics, but he did tolerate them. "I'm from the generation that says, 'Son, don't flaunt yourself,'" Bowden said. But the coach knew that football had changed from the old days. "The nature is to showboat," he said. "I'd rather you not, but we want to keep the enthusiasm of the game, keep the excitement."

Sanders certainly had plenty of help in keeping the excitement alive for the 'Noles in the 1980s. Players such as

ALL-AMERICAN RON

SIMMONS (ABOVE);

RECORD-BREAKING BACK

WARRICK DUNN (BELOW)

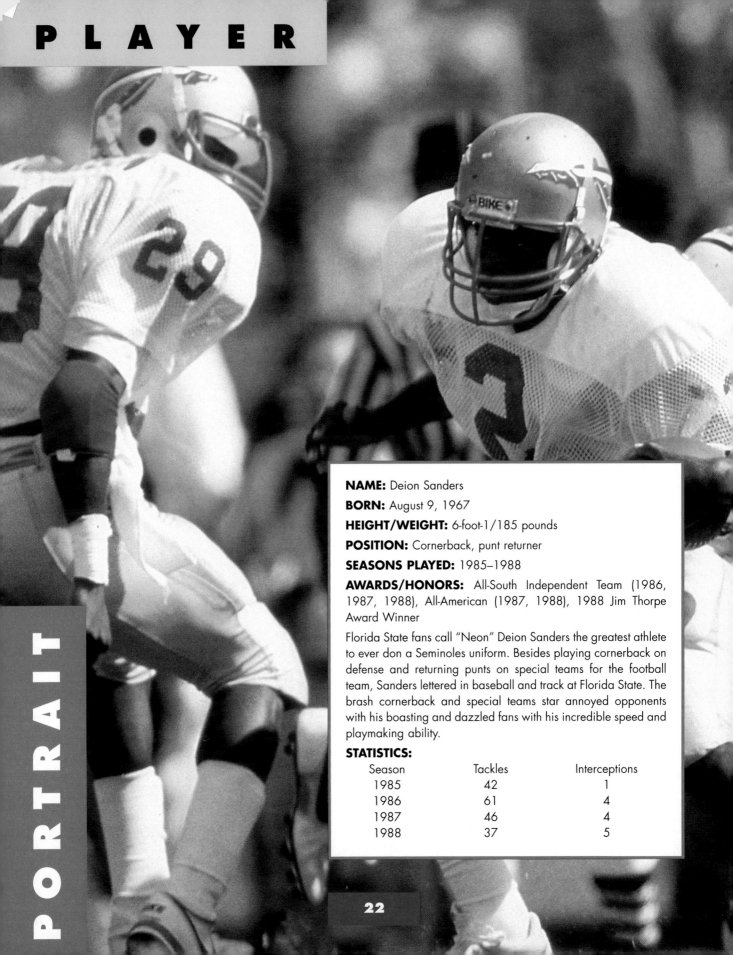

NAME: Deion Sanders

BORN: August 9, 1967

HEIGHT/WEIGHT: 6-foot-1/185 pounds

POSITION: Cornerback, punt returner

SEASONS PLAYED: 1985–1988

AWARDS/HONORS: All-South Independent Team (1986, 1987, 1988), All-American (1987, 1988), 1988 Jim Thorpe Award Winner

Florida State fans call "Neon" Deion Sanders the greatest athlete to ever don a Seminoles uniform. Besides playing cornerback on defense and returning punts on special teams for the football team, Sanders lettered in baseball and track at Florida State. The brash cornerback and special teams star annoyed opponents with his boasting and dazzled fans with his incredible speed and playmaking ability.

STATISTICS:

Season	Tackles	Interceptions
1985	42	1
1986	61	4
1987	46	4
1988	37	5

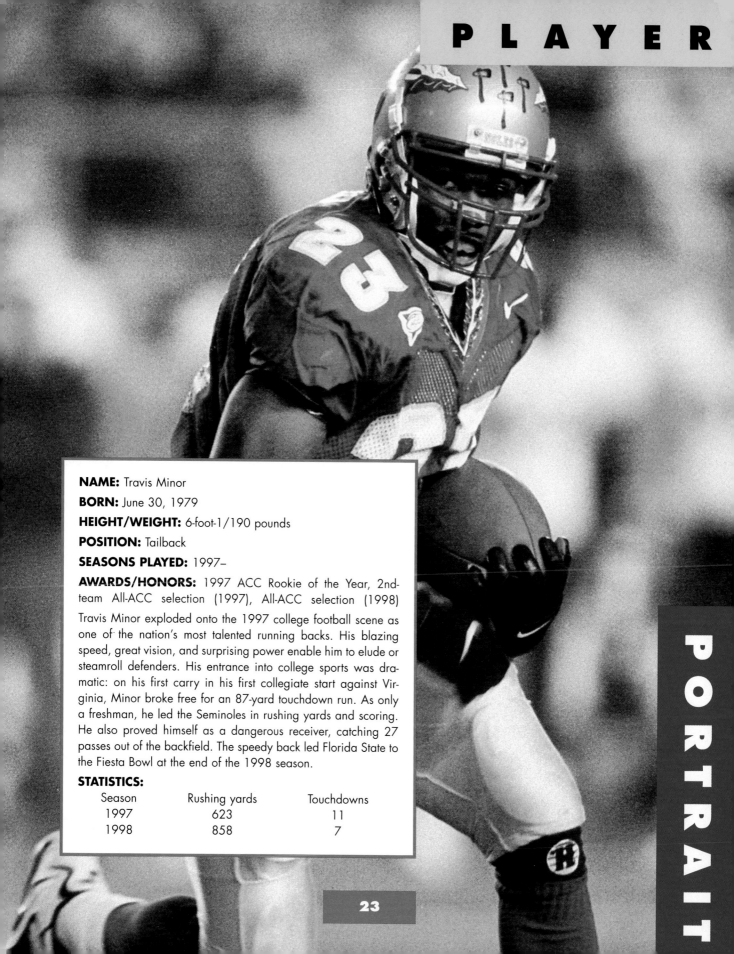

NAME: Travis Minor

BORN: June 30, 1979

HEIGHT/WEIGHT: 6-foot-1/190 pounds

POSITION: Tailback

SEASONS PLAYED: 1997–

AWARDS/HONORS: 1997 ACC Rookie of the Year, 2nd-team All-ACC selection (1997), All-ACC selection (1998)

Travis Minor exploded onto the 1997 college football scene as one of the nation's most talented running backs. His blazing speed, great vision, and surprising power enable him to elude or steamroll defenders. His entrance into college sports was dramatic: on his first carry in his first collegiate start against Virginia, Minor broke free for an 87-yard touchdown run. As only a freshman, he led the Seminoles in rushing yards and scoring. He also proved himself as a dangerous receiver, catching 27 passes out of the backfield. The speedy back led Florida State to the Fiesta Bowl at the end of the 1998 season.

STATISTICS:

Season	Rushing yards	Touchdowns
1997	623	11
1998	858	7

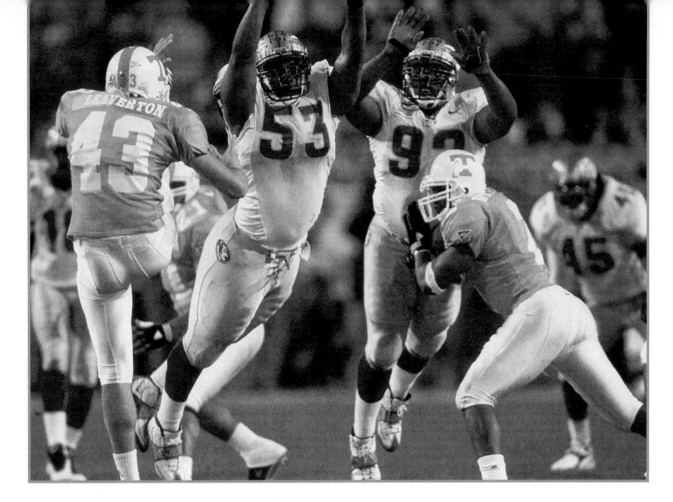

tailback Greg Allen, offensive guard Jamie Dukes, quarterback Danny McManus, and linebacker Paul McGowan, who won the Butkus Award as the nation's best college linebacker in 1987, kept the wins coming by the barrelful. The Seminoles' 88–28–3 record in the '80s represents an astounding winning percentage of .752. Bowden's boys went to nine bowl games during the decade and posted a remarkable 6–2–1 record.

Neon Deion finished his FSU career with 14 career interceptions and went on to become the only professional athlete to ever play in both the Super Bowl (with the San Francisco 49ers) and the World Series (with the Atlanta Braves).

ALL-AMERICAN ROOMMATES

Up until 1993, Bobby Bowden had done everything there was to do in college football except bring Florida State a national title. "We had been close a number of times but just couldn't get over the hump," explained the coach. The final pieces to the championship puzzle fell into place when quarterback Charlie Ward and tailback Warrick Dunn took the field.

Before his 1993 Heisman Trophy-winning season, Ward, the team's senior All-American quarterback, agreed to take the freshman Dunn in as a roommate. Dunn's mother, a police officer, had been murdered in Baton Rouge during her son's senior year in high school. Warrick, the oldest of six children, wanted to stay home to care for his brothers and sisters rather than play football. However, a family friend convinced Dunn to go to college to play football and continue his education.

Former NFL quarterback Doug Williams, a friend of Dunn, asked Ward to look after Warrick while he was at Florida State. Ward gladly agreed. The soft-spoken young men got along wonderfully, in part because they both believed in letting their on-field actions speak for themselves.

In 1993, Ward's actions spoke loudly. He completed a Florida State-record 264 passes for 3,032 yards and 27 touchdowns. He also led the Seminoles to a heart-stopping, 18–16 victory over the Nebraska Cornhuskers in the Orange Bowl, dodging disaster when Nebraska's last-second field goal attempt sailed wide left.

BIG QUARTERBACKS BRAD

JOHNSON (ABOVE) AND

CHRIS WEINKE (BELOW)

With that victory, Florida State ended their season at 12–1 and locked up the national championship.

As soon as the long season ended, Ward picked up a basketball and slid into his starting spot as Florida State's point guard. As his senior year ended, Ward had a decision to make: would he play football in the NFL or basketball in the National Basketball Association? Although ESPN's color commentator Lee Corso called Ward "the best quarterback I've seen since Roger Staubach," Ward chose basketball.

After Ward's departure from Florida State, Warrick Dunn emerged as the Seminoles' star. Despite coaches' efforts to change him into a defensive back, Dunn remained firm in his desire to be a tailback. Dunn's high school coach, Dale Weiner, told the Florida State coaching staff, "Warrick will be great wherever you play him, but believe me, he's a special running back. You can't catch this guy in a phone booth."

No one could catch Dunn in his years at FSU. He smashed Florida State's career rushing record with 3,959 yards and its scoring record with 49 touchdowns. He is the only Seminoles player to ever rush for more than 1,000 yards in three straight seasons. In 1999, Dunn began his third season in the NFL with the Tampa Bay Buccaneers, able to provide nicely for his five brothers and sisters.

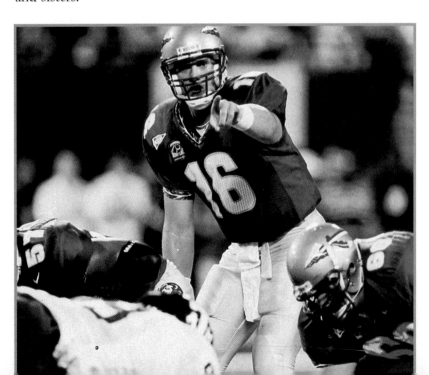

WARRICK AND WEINKE TAKE TO THE AIR

The passing game has always held a special place in the hearts of FSU fans. Although most schools shunned the pass and stuck to conservative ground attacks for years, Bowden's offenses revolved around the throwing game. "I never could find the logic in recruiting a lot of fast, talented players and then pounding them into the line of scrimmage," explained Bowden. "I believe yards and points come easier through the air."

Florida State's aerial attack during much of the 1998 season was powered by two talented players. Twenty-one-year-old junior wide receiver Peter Warrick and 26-year-old sophomore quarterback Chris Weinke may not have been close in age, but on the field they were of one mind—attack at all times.

In 1989, as a high school senior in St. Paul, Minnesota, Weinke was the nation's most highly rated quarterback. He signed with the Seminoles but then decided to play professional baseball for the Toronto Blue Jays. Coach Bowden wished him luck and told him that Florida State's scholarship would still be open if he ever changed his mind.

After spending six frustrating years in Toronto's minor-league system, Weinke realized that he might never make it to the major-league level. He decided to take Bowden up on his offer and headed to Florida State.

Despite the age gap between Weinke and his teammates, the quarterback believes that his maturity helps him as the team's leader. "I'm older than these guys," acknowledged Weinke. "I want them to know I'm willing to lead, willing to say something when things aren't going right."

AN 11–2 RECORD IN 1998 KEPT SEMINOLES FLAGS FLYING HIGH.

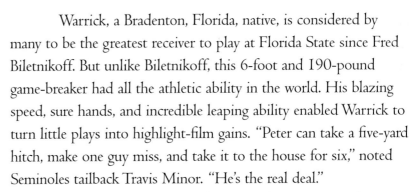

Warrick, a Bradenton, Florida, native, is considered by many to be the greatest receiver to play at Florida State since Fred Biletnikoff. But unlike Biletnikoff, this 6-foot and 190-pound game-breaker had all the athletic ability in the world. His blazing speed, sure hands, and incredible leaping ability enabled Warrick to turn little plays into highlight-film gains. "Peter can take a five-yard hitch, make one guy miss, and take it to the house for six," noted Seminoles tailback Travis Minor. "He's the real deal."

Warrick exploded onto the national scene as a sophomore, catching 53 passes for 884 yards and eight touchdowns. He also returned 29 punts for a 13.4 yard average, including a dazzling, 90-yard return for a touchdown against Clemson. No one appreciated his talents more than Weinke. "It makes my job as quarterback a lot easier knowing that, if we get in a tough situation, I can just throw it up, and Peter will go get it," he said.

POWERFUL KICKER

SEBASTIAN JANIKOWSKI

(ABOVE); RECEIVER PETER

WARRICK (BELOW)

FIGHTING FOR THE TOP

The Florida State University football team begins every season with the realistic goal of winning a national championship. "There's no question that Florida State is a dynasty," wrote Tim Layden of *Sports Illustrated* in 1998. The second-ranked Seminoles were hoping to build on this dynasty when they faced the top-ranked Tennessee Volunteers in the 1999 Fiesta Bowl—the

1999 CHAMPIONSHIP GAME

national championship game under the newly instated Bowl Championship Series format.

With Weinke sidelined with a neck injury, Marcus Outzen made only his third start at quarterback for the 11-1 'Noles. Although the game was a tight defensive struggle, Florida State came up short to the undefeated Volunteers, 23–16. Multiple turnovers, 110 yards in penalties, the Vols' relentless pressure on Outzen, and an off-game by game-breaker Peter Warrick doomed the Seminoles' championship dreams. Despite the disappointing loss, Florida State pushed to 12 its incredible streak of seasons with at least 10 wins and a final national ranking of fourth or higher.

With Weinke returning to spearhead the Seminoles' offensive attack, FSU shows no signs of losing its title as college football's most consistently explosive team. Talented players such as ultra-quick tailback Travis Minor, linebacker Tommy Polley, and strong-legged kicker Sebastion Janikowski appear more than capable of keeping Florida State among the nation's elite programs.

With Bowden in place to guide the ferocious 'Noles into the future, more championship seasons seem likely in Tallahassee. "I like the group of young men I've got here," said Bowden. "They have talent, for sure, but I see a lot of character and heart in this bunch. We're a young team, but this team's best football is ahead of it."